Meet ...
everyone from

TURBO RACING TEAM

Theo and Chet are snails. They live in a garden. They are brothers.

Chet

Theo

This is **Guy Gagné**. He is a racing driver. His car has a turbo engine. It is very fast.

Guy Gagné

Tito and **Angelo** are brothers too. They work in Starlight Plaza.

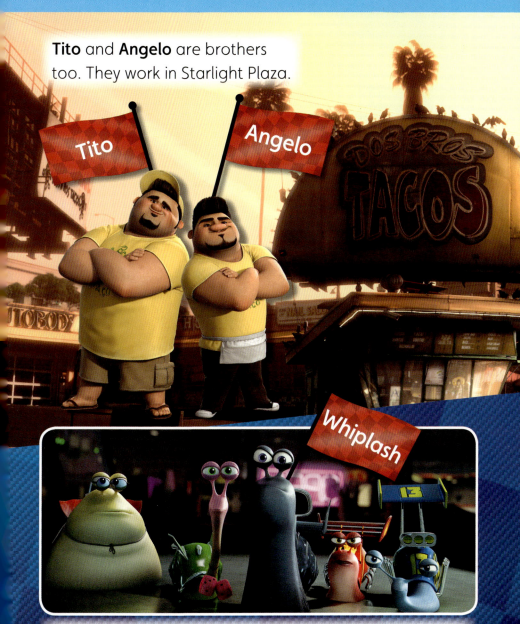

Whiplash and his friends are snails. They live in the city.

> Before you read …
> What do you think? Who likes to win races?

New Words

What do these new words mean? Ask your teacher or use your dictionary.

different

These socks are **different**.

accident

The car had an **accident**.

dream

The girl has a **dream**.

city

It is a big **city**.

drive / driver

She is **driving**. / She is the **driver**.

engine

race

The are in a **race**. / They are **racing**.

fast

The car is **fast**.

win / winner

She is **winning**. / She is the **winner**.

money

This is **money**.

'What's the matter?'

Verbs

Present	Past
drive	drove
fall	fell
take	took

What does *Turbo* mean? Ask your teacher.

CHAPTER ONE
Theo's dream

Theo was a snail. He lived in a garden with his brother, Chet. Every day, Chet and Theo worked with the garden snails but Theo was never happy.

'What's the matter?' asked Chet.

'I want to do something different,' said Theo.

Every night, Theo watched car races on TV. Guy Gagné was his favourite racing driver.

'My dream is to win races,' said Guy. 'You can have your dream too!'

Theo had a dream. He wanted to race.

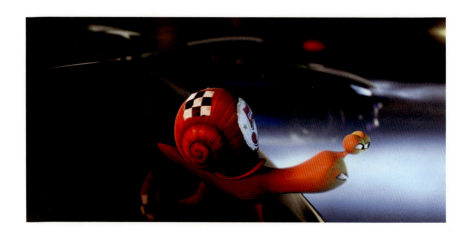

One night, Theo went to the city. He wanted to see some cars. He jumped on a car and it started to race. The car drove very fast and Theo fell into the turbo engine. When Theo came out of the engine, he was different.

'I'm a turbo snail now!' he said.

CHAPTER TWO
In the city

'Look at me!' Theo said to Chet.
   But Chet was angry.
   'What's the matter?' asked Theo.
   'You are not a car, you're a snail!' said Chet.
   Suddenly a big bird took Chet away.
   'Theo! Help me!' shouted Chet.

The bird went to the city. Theo raced to find Chet. Chet fell onto the road but Theo saw him.

'Hey, Chet!' he shouted.

'Oh, Theo! Thank you, brother,' answered Chet.

'This place is horrible,' said Chet. 'Let's go home to the garden.'

Suddenly they saw a man. The man was Tito.

'Hello, small snails,' he said and he took them away.

Chet and Theo were very frightened.

Tito took the snails to Starlight Plaza. Every night at Starlight Plaza, there was a race ... a snail race.

Theo and Chet were in the race. Theo went very fast and he was first.

Theo was very happy. Tito was happy too.

The city snails were cool.

'Hello, garden snails,' said one of the snails. 'My name's Whiplash and these are my friends.'

Theo looked at the city snails. They were racing snails. He wanted a racing name too.

'My name's Turbo!' he said.

CHAPTER THREE
Tito's dream

Tito wanted to win a big race.

'This snail is fast,' he said to his friends in the shops of Starlight Plaza. 'It can win a car race!'

'But I have no money for a car race,' said Tito sadly.

'We can help!' said Whiplash.

The city snails stopped a bus. Everyone on the bus went to Starlight Plaza. They went into all the shops and they watched a snail race. They loved Turbo!

Tito's friends were very happy. Now they had some money to help Tito.

'We're going to win!' said Tito. 'We're going to the Indy 500!'

Tito looked for Angelo. But Angelo was not happy.

'What's the matter, Angelo?' Tito asked.

'A snail can't win a car race,' said Angelo.

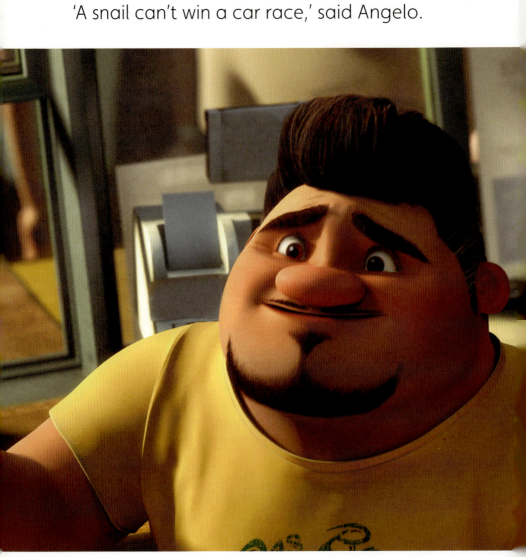

Chet was not happy about the race.
'What's the matter, Chet?' Turbo asked.
'A snail can't win the Indy 500,' said Chet.
'I'm going to win!' said Turbo. 'I'm a turbo snail now!'

CHAPTER FOUR
The Indy 500

Tito and his friends went to Indiana for the Indy 500 race with Guy Gagné.

'This is my racing driver,' said Tito.

'Can a snail race with cars?' asked Guy Gagné.

'He's very fast,' said Tito. 'Look!'

Everyone watched Turbo. Everyone loved him.

'Hey!' said Guy Gagné. 'I want to race with the snail!'

Turbo was very happy. 'I'm going to race with Guy Gagné,' he said.

In the evening, Turbo saw Guy again.

'Listen, snail,' said Guy. He was angry. 'You are not going to win this race. Everyone is here to see ME!'

Turbo was sad. 'He's not my favourite racing driver now,' he said.

CHAPTER FIVE
Race day

It was time for the race. All the racing drivers were at the start.

'Hello everyone, it's time for the Indy 500!' said the man on TV. 'Today we have a new racing driver. It's Turbo the snail!'

The race started. The cars were very fast and very big. Turbo was frightened but everyone shouted, 'Go, Turbo, go!'

Chet was very frightened too. He did not want to watch the race.

Turbo drove fast. He drove under the cars. Now he was in front!

Guy was very angry. 'I'm going to stop you, snail!' he shouted. But then …

Bang! Crash! There was a big accident.

Turbo had a problem.

'I'm not a turbo snail now,' he said.

But everyone shouted, 'Go, Turbo, go!'

'I can do it!' said Turbo. He went very slowly.

'I'm going to win!' shouted Guy Gagné. But Guy had a problem with his car.

Guy was behind Turbo.
'You can't stop me now!' said Turbo.
'Look!' shouted everyone. 'Turbo is the winner!'
'That's my brother!' said Chet.
'This is my dream!' said Turbo.

THE END

Real World

All about snails

Turbo and his friends are snails.
Snails can be very small or very big.

Land snails

Some snails live on land. Land snails eat plants. They eat at night or when it is rainy. Land snails can't hear. They can't see very much. They smell their food.

The giant African land snail can be 20 cm long!

Water snails

Water snails live in the sea or in rivers. They eat water plants or small animals.

Water snails can be 10 mm long!

Snail shells

Some snails have very beautiful shells. Young snails have small shells. The shell grows with the snail.

Did you know?

Snails live for about 5 years. Some snails live for more than 20 years.

Do you like snails? Why? / Why not?

What do these words mean? Find out.
land   plant   smell   river   grow

After you read

1 Match the names and the sentences.

a) Chet
b) Whiplash
c) Angelo
d) Turbo
e) Guy Gagné
f) Tito

i) is Tito's brother.
ii) has a very fast car.
iii) wins the race.
iv) is a city snail.
v) finds Theo and Chet.
vi) is Turbo's brother.

2 Circle the correct word.

a) Theo and Chet were (garden) / city snails.
b) Angelo and Tito worked at Indy 500 / Starlight Plaza.
c) Theo fell into the road / a turbo engine.
d) Guy was nice / horrible to Turbo.
e) Turbo came first / second in the Indy 500.

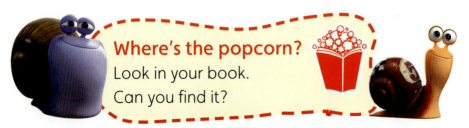

Where's the popcorn?
Look in your book.
Can you find it?

Puzzle time!

1 Read, colour and write.

The orange snail is in front of the green snail.
The blue snail is behind the green snail.
The yellow snail is behind the blue snail.
The red snail is in front of the orange snail.

Which snail is first? ....

2 Find six more words.

PHOTOCOPIABLE

3 Look at the pictures. Write *fast* or *slow*.

1  2  3

slow ....

4  5  6

....

4 Find four more mistakes.

a) Yesterday Turbo the snail came ~~second~~ **first** in a car race.

b) 'I'm the winner of the Indy 300!' he said.

c) Gary Gagné came second in his red racing bus.

d) 'I am very happy,' said Turbo's sister, Chet.

30

Imagine ...

1 Imagine you are Guy Gagné after the race. Answer the questions.

Did you win the race?

Was it a good race?

Are you happy?

Do you like snails?

2 Now imagine you are Turbo after the race. Answer the questions.

Did you win the race?

Was it a good race?

Are you happy?

Do you like Guy Gagné?

3 Work in pairs. Act out the interviews.

Chant

1 Listen and read.

Go, Turbo, go!

Turbo isn't happy,
Oh no, no, no!
He's a garden snail,
He is slow, slow, slow.

One day he is different,
Not slow, slow, slow.
Tito wants a winner
And they go, go, go!

Gagné wants to stop him,
But no, no, no!
Turbo is the winner,
Go, Turbo, go!

2 Say the chant.